HOW TO HELP THE PLANET

BUILDING HABITS TO HELP EARTH

by
Rebecca Phillips-Bartlett

Minneapolis, Minnesota

Credits: All images are courtesy of Shutterstock.com, unless otherwise specified. With thanks to Getty Images, Thinkstock Photo, and iStockphoto. Recurring images – VectorMine, Anna Kosheleva. Cover – VectorMine, Monkey Business Images. 2–3 – Evgeny Atamanenko. 4–5 – alphaspirit.it, SUKJAI PHOTO. 6–7 – rangizzz, Waridsara_HappyChildren. 8–9 – Antonina Vlasova, Black Salmon. 10–11 – MOHAMED ABDULRAHEEM, Warongdech Digital, Alexey Kartsev. 12–13 – Victoria 1, Russamee. 14–15 – Hurst Photo, Lithiumphoto. 16–17 – Irina Wilhauk, J.M. Image Factory. 18–19 – Gary Whitton, Monkey Business Images, TonyV3112. 20–21 – DGLimages, max dallocco. 22–23 – vovidzha, Irina Wilhauk.

Bearport Publishing Company Product Development Team
President: Jen Jenson; Director of Product Development: Spencer Brinker; Managing Editor: Allison Juda; Associate Editor: Naomi Reich; Associate Editor: Tiana Tran; Senior Designer: Colin O'Dea; Designer: Elena Klinkner; Designer: Kayla Eggert; Product Development Assistant: Owen Hamlin

Library of Congress Cataloging-in-Publication Data is available at www.loc.gov or upon request from the publisher.

ISBN: 979-8-88916-286-5 (hardcover)
ISBN: 979-8-88916-291-9 (paperback)
ISBN: 979-8-88916-295-7 (ebook)

© 2024 BookLife Publishing
This edition is published by arrangement with BookLife Publishing.

North American adaptations © 2024 Bearport Publishing Company. All rights reserved. No part of this publication may be reproduced in whole or in part, stored in any retrieval system, or transmitted in any form or by any means, electronic, mechanical, photocopying, recording, or otherwise, without written permission from the publisher.

For more information, write to Bearport Publishing, 5357 Penn Avenue South, Minneapolis, MN 55419.

CONTENTS

Our Planet, Our Home 4
There Is Plenty We Can Do 6
What Is a Carbon Footprint? 8
How to Reduce 10
How to Reuse 12
How to Recycle 14
How to Travel 16
How to Save Electricity 18
How to Save Water 20
We Can Help 22
Glossary 24
Index 24

OUR PLANET, OUR HOME

Earth is our home. It gives us everything we need to live. The planet takes care of us, but we are not always good at taking care of it.

Over the years, Earth has been getting hotter because of things people do. This shift in temperature is a part of **climate change**. The heat hurts the planet and the living things on it.

Climate change is a shift in the usual weather of a place.

THERE IS PLENTY
WE CAN DO

Climate change is a problem, but there is plenty we can do to help Earth. Even the smallest things can make a difference.

The things we do every day, such as brushing our teeth or exercising, are called habits. Having good habits is a great way to help the planet. Let's make habits to fight climate change!

Doing something every day makes it a habit.

WHAT IS A CARBON FOOTPRINT?

One thing that causes climate change is too many **greenhouse gases**. These gases trap heat on the planet. A **carbon footprint** measures the amount of these gases a person's actions put into the air.

Driving our cars and heating our homes lets out greenhouse gases.

Our habits affect the size of our carbon footprint. The things we eat, the ways we travel, and how we get rid of used things can make our footprint bigger or smaller.

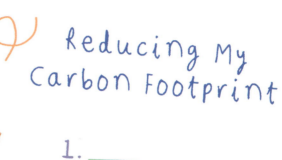

Reducing My Carbon Footprint

1. _____
2. _____
3. _____

HOW TO
REDUCE

Factories make a lot of greenhouse gases.

If we have or use fewer things, we can make our carbon footprint smaller. That is because making new things lets out greenhouse gases. Some things we buy are made in factories. Try to **reduce** the number of things you get.

When we throw things away, this trash gets sent to **landfills**. These places make a lot of greenhouse gases, too. Before throwing something out, get into the habit of using it as much as you can.

A LANDFILL

Will I play with this a lot before I'm finished with it?

HOW TO REUSE

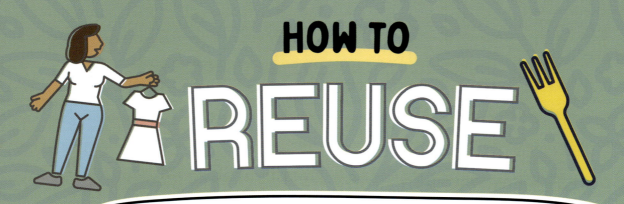

What we **reuse** can help the planet, too. Some things, such as paper plates and plastic straws, are made to be used once. Then, these **single-use** items are sent to landfills.

Hmm, what else could I use this for?

Make a list of items we can reuse many times.

Make a habit of carrying a reusable water bottle. When you grow out of clothes, give them to someone else who can use them.

13

HOW TO RECYCLE

Not everything can be reused. But we can still get rid of things in a way that helps the planet. If we **recycle** things, they can be made into something new!

With an adult, find out what you can recycle in your area. Make a poster showing what you can and cannot recycle.

We can recycle cardboard, paper, and metal cans in most places.

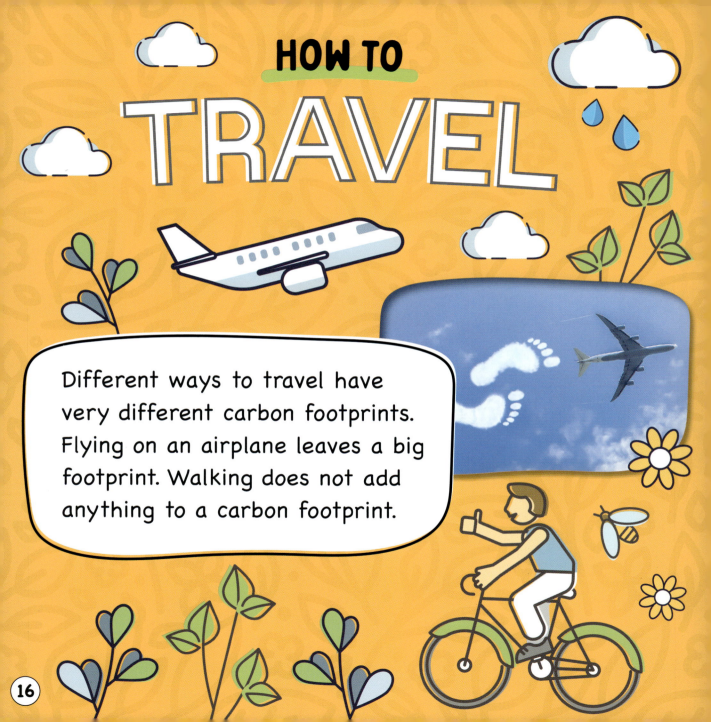

If school is too far away to walk, share car rides with friends.

Even changing how we take short trips can have a big impact on our carbon footprint. Make a habit of walking or biking to school.

HOW TO SAVE ELECTRICITY

We use electricity all the time. It powers our lights, televisions, and microwaves. But making electricity can be bad for the planet.

A POWER PLANT

As **power plants** make electricity, they put out a lot of greenhouse gases.

Form simple habits to save electricity! Turn the lights off when you leave a room. Unplug things you are not using, such as chargers.

HOW TO SAVE WATER

Most of Earth is covered in water, but there is only a small amount that we can use. Make a habit of saving water so that we do not run out!

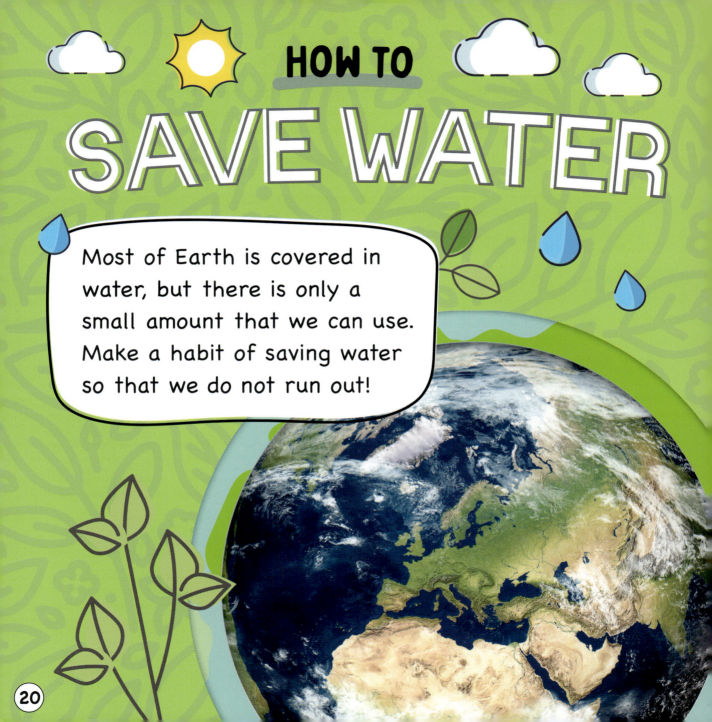

Saving water helps make a carbon footprint smaller, too. Turn off the water when brushing your teeth. Take a shower instead of a bath.

Brushing your teeth with the tap running wastes about 4 gallons (15 L) of water.

WE CAN HELP

Climate change is a problem for our planet. However, good habits can make a big difference and keep our carbon footprints small.

It takes time to build habits. But once they form, they stay with us for a long time. Build good habits now, and you will help the planet for years!

Which habit will you start first?

GLOSSARY

carbon footprint a measure of the carbon dioxide and other gases released into the air because of a person's activities

climate change the change to Earth's weather patterns

greenhouse gases gases that trap heat around Earth

landfills large holes in the ground used for dumping trash

power plants factories that make electricity

recycle to turn something old into something new

reduce to use less

reuse to use again

single-use something made to be used once before it is thrown away or recycled

INDEX

carbon footprints 8–10, 16–17, 21–22
climate change 5–8, 22
clothes 13
Earth 4–6, 20
electricity 18–19
greenhouse gases 8, 10–11, 18
habits 7, 9, 11, 13, 17, 19–20, 22–23
lights 18–19
trash 11
water 13, 20–21